she doesn't seem autistic

she doesn't seem autistic

Esther Ottaway

PUNCHER & WATTMANN

First published in 2023
Published by Puncher and Wattmann
PO Box 279
Waratah NSW 2298

https://www.puncherandwattmann.com
web@puncherandwattmann.com

ISBN   9781922571762

Cover image by Esther Ottaway
Cover design by Miranda Douglas
Typesetting by Morgan Arnett
Printed by Lightning Source International

 A catalogue record for this work is available from the National Library of Australia

Acknowledgements

Poems from this collection have been published, some in slightly different forms, in *Rattle, Australian Poetry Journal, Meanjin, Cordite, Island, Live Encounters Poetry & Writing, Burrow, Raging Grace: Australian writers speak out on disability*, and at *redroompoetry.org*, and have won the Queensland Poetry Festival QRAA Flying Arts Alliance Ekphrasis Prize 2021, second prize in the Fellowship of Australian Writers Colin & Norma Knight Memorial Award 2021, third prize in the MPU International Poetry Competition 2022, and been shortlisted in the Mslexia International Poetry Competition (UK).

After writing a book on female autism, I decide to bury it is part of a poem pair written with Andy Jackson. *Field notes from the autistic seahorse* uses factual statements from the iSeahorse.org web archive. *Elegy for a fun childhood* uses the words "I am a door wide/open" from Zeina Issa's poem *Blemish-less. There is always a giraffe* is after Judy Johnson. *[working memory]* takes the line "The slate is a slate and not a page" from Melinda Smith's poem *Slippage. The shamed body addresses its owner* is part of a poem pair written with Rachael Wenona Guy. *Shaky underpinnings* is a response to *Discordant song of my becoming* by Rachael Wenona Guy. The terms *Can't Keep House Woman and Man* are inspired by Claire Delahunty's *Go Home Woman. girl brains mean nothing* is after Kerri Shying and uses lines and images from her poetry collection, *Knitting Mangrove Roots. Yes* is after W.S Merwin. *Still I rise: female autism* is after Maya Angelou. *Joy to my world* is part of a poem pair written with Kerri Shying. *For I will consider the delightfulness of my grown daughter* is after Christopher Smart.

I thank David Musgrave and Morgan Arnett of Puncher & Wattmann, Jacinta Le Plastrier, Melinda Smith, Susan Austin, Gina Mercer, Ralph Wessman, John Foulcher, Lyn Reeves, Karen Knight, Andy Jackson, Kim Nolan and my sister, Amelie, who all supported the making of this book in various, generous ways. My thanks also to each of the editors who selected these poems for publication in their literary journals.

This project has been assisted by the Australian Government through the Australia Council for the Arts, its arts funding and advisory body. It was also supported by RANT Arts (Regional Arts Australia). My thanks to those on the assessment panels who saw value in this project.

Contents

Foreword

It is not known what the true prevalence of autism is in women, because studies were done on boys, and diagnostic criteria came from those studies. This is typical of what researcher Caroline Criado Perez terms the "gender data gap."[1] This data gap about women is vast: a search on the bookselling site Amazon returns just twenty books on autism in women – in the world.

Women with autism find it as disabling as men do, likely more so, since social expectations of women are much higher; but women are usually without diagnosis, let alone assistance. They present differently to men, though not that differently: much of the problem with getting women diagnosed lies in a gender stereotype which says that they can't be autistic.

Through a diagnostic journey with my daughter, I have realised, in recent years, that the autism spectrum explains the severe difficulties I've had all my life. Perhaps, reading me as socially competent, you could think my autism merely gives me a different way of seeing the world. In truth, it's a profound, continuous disruption to my physical health, senses, coordination, memory, and power to act. I'm not fundamentally healthy with occasional difficulties; I'm fundamentally unwell and dysregulated, with occasional high points. I was born with fatigue-related health and nervous conditions that defied diagnosis, particularly when weighed against my intelligence. As well as its social, mental and emotional impacts, autistic women and children are sick with physical conditions: almost all autistic people have chronic health conditions, and nearly half of us, including me, are dealing with six conditions or more. Autistic people live shorter lives.

For women, of whom much is expected socially, showing the traits of autism is so shameful that they learn early to hide them. I'm a member of Generation X, which is described as "self-sufficient, results-oriented and

---

1. The gender data gap is a term coined by Caroline Criado Perez in her book, *Invisible Women: Exposing Data Bias in a World Designed For Men*.

hard-working": a generation which saw disability as failure, illness as weakness. Nor is Australian culture one where you talk about disability. Autistic girls study, by reading books, watching movies and copying others, how to mask their deficits and differences. That's exhausting, and leads to breakdowns. I had a breakdown at nineteen.

I've lived through the difficulty of managing these complex autism spectrum conditions in myself and my daughter, and battling to get them recognised in a system designed for boys. The demands of this management became so high that I all but stopped socialising – as well as writing – for eight years. By the age of forty, I was tired of feeling actively dishonest when I answered *"good!"* to the question, *"how are you?"* How I am is incredibly complex, and it takes this book to give an answer. It strengthened my resolve when the idea of this book was endorsed as an important one by the Literature Board of the Australia Council, RANT Arts, and Puncher & Wattmann, who all gave their immediate support.

You will naturally wonder how many of these poems reflect my own life. It is many more than you might think. Yet, I gathered the experiences of a range of autistic women and girls for this book, creating a composite woman and girl. This has allowed me to keep private exactly what my experience entails. And there are still other experiences not covered here.

I take this opportunity to recommend to autistic women a neuroplasticity practice which helps me to feel social and sensory enjoyment: information on it is found at retrainingthebrain.com.

I want, through these poems, to show you a profile of autism that you are not familiar with: an autistic girl and woman. Please allow her to exist, in your mind, and in the world around you.

Now, there are twenty-one books.

After writing a book on female autism, I decide to bury it

Go on with that public Esther, curated pretence:
to be and not to be, that is Australian.

What good are these chalk traces around spent victims?
Why lift the sheet on myself, fatigued, confounded?

I know what I'd be next: that bleating woman,
the car alarm that barely registers.

Truth-pregnant, I laboured. Her name is Repercussions.
My fear: that this child kicks, draws breath to cry.

There's no disabled girls with style like mine

A woman wearing makeup must be fine.
They tell me *there is nothing wrong with you.*
Disabled girls cannot have style like mine.

Good-looking girls are not supposed to whine
or carry on about what they can't do.
A woman wearing makeup must be fine

and healthy, strong, except when her waistline
is big: then the first thing she needs to do
is lose that weight. No girls with style like mine

have hidden disabilities, or climb
up mountains of distress. From birth, we knew
that little girls in dresses must be fine

and happy. When I talk about decline,
my sobbing, shattered meltdowns, self-harm, blue
nights, they fail to see, through style like mine,

my terrors, my self-medicating wine.
I dress well and it helps my grip stay true
on mental health. My fault for looking fine.

You're clearly well, don't waste the doctor's time.
Autistics do not look the way you do.
A woman wearing makeup must be fine.
There's no disabled girls with style like mine.

Field notes on the autistic seahorse

The hippocampus is affected in autism, with severe impacts on the fight-or-flight response, motivation and emotion. It is also the name for seahorses.

young are the most vulnerable
    acid-burnt by sensory life
        cross between being dissected and being boiled
            high-salinity waters
                nightly sobbing
                    the hot humiliation of the end of my rope
colour changes occur during daily greetings
    people panic me, trigger me to say
        things I don't even believe
            chameleon without consent
                flapping pectoral fins, terror-black pupils
                    unremarked syntax of distress
data is lacking on seahorse populations
    the only one in the seagrass
        couple of nerds at primary school
            high school the few intellectual girls
                every adult woman I knew going swimmingly
                    google seahorses, there's almost nothing
seahorses are not good swimmers, so they need to anchor themselves
    death-grip on microhabitat
        same job same town same home same food
            long to surf thrill-waves of variety
                but prying open my deadlocked tail
                    fatally cracks my bones

seahorses are masters of camouflage
you with your fish-gutting words
I'll say what you want switch my flush of identifying marks
just stop picking on me laughing at me
today I'm the spitting image of the seabed
incredible at not being there

Hippocampus zosterae
slowest-moving of all fish
five feet in an hour
can't make it to the shower
handwritten self-care notes
illegible in a press of ocean

seahorses exhibit almost no signs of distress
distress arrests the mechanics
of my ability to speak
so I can't tell you I'm perennially distressed
all statuesque exoskeleton
seahorses are so serene

while seahorses appear to be very different from other fish, they are fish nonetheless
radio waves are made of light
an earthquake is actually sound
in hermetic bays, between roots, drifting vegetation
I hold my secrets, beige-black, emerald, stone
come swim beside me under invisible stars

The viola d'amore on why she avoids conversation
Empathy overarousal in autism

Too highly strung, and speech is vellicate:
      every note of mild concern in your voice
            amplified in my sympathetic strings.

They do not require playing: made of gut instinct
      each augments vibrations, as I hear the matters of your life
            and loved ones, who's in care, whose cancer's going badly –

here your griefs enter my delicate sprucewood
      as oscillation, as finely-tuned carnivorous birds
            to later swoop, to tear, in the cage of my skin,

in my head carved into unbearably vulnerable Cupid,
      his eyes covered against weldschmertz. I am unfretted
            but how I fret, your lacks and losses louder in my nerves

than in your own: here the sound-wounds in my body
      open in shapes of flaming swords. How I cannot bear,
            as Mozart said, the stillness of the evening, the swelling

harmonics of distress, until the pains of thousands
      cry through me in agonised haloes. I cannot come near
            your troubles. I must love you deaf, afar.

Tigridia

Rejection sensitive dysphoria

Tigridia, shell flower, I bloom
on meeting you. Our conversation sparks;
I shine, three-petalled lily, in the room,
my chat bright, lively. Tall and tiger-marked,
I unfurl at your friendship for one day,
a speckle-patterned time-bomb at my heart –
then, in the early evening, shut away
never to open again. Bleak voices start:
relentless, vicious insecurity,
rejection's sureness, shame. All night I lie
in the distressing electricity
of tender stamens curling back to die.
A thousand cowed antennae on my brain.
Killed bloom, can't bear to get in touch again.

Dysavowal: the basic human emotions
Alexithymia, empathy overarousal, situational mutism

The six human emotions
are universally experienced
in all human cultures
but mine.

My lexicon:
happiness-terror
sadness-terror
anger-terror
surprise-terror
fear-terror
disgust-terror.

Not a gradient,
a vortex.
When the fall doesn't kill me
it's the excruciating
climb back up.
Can't go there
without a helmet, caving gear,
rations, maps,
a knife between my teeth.

Intensity
strikes me mute –
system floods,
shuts down.
Silence is the sound of survival.
Don't tell me your words mean the same as mine.

I will not summon those darknesses
speaking them into being.
I've grabbed words by both their arms,
thrown them off that crumbling ledge,
listened to them echo.

Miss Communication
Masking, echolalia, situational mutism, ADHD

rehearsal
medication
intense concentration
a butterfly can fly
with seventy percent of its wings missing

I'm not stupid; I know
women have to be seen as talkers
bubbly personality in every job description

my genes know how: great-great Aunt Alice
was the life of incredible parties
then would take to bed, silent, for days

could everyone please notice that autistic men often talk
a little bit too long
a little bit too loud
so can I: audio tour of my head's exhibits
each word the same each time

my name is Echolalia
talk easily, I'll talk easily
talk haltingly, I'll talk haltingly
you're talking with yourself

hearing speech plus everything else acutely
is pain
death metal concert
during a medical procedure

        don't tell them what I really think
        especially when they say *tell me what you really think*
        too blunt too cutting too bottom-line
        alarmed shoals scattering

                am I talking, or just saying
                  yes   oh   right   wow
                to the talking you're doing?
        how easily that passes for conversation

      secret button on my ADHD
      in the right cranial weather I can talk flat out
      sharing much more than I wanted to
      mouth spilling coins

I'm talking out my intellect
can't make you feel my feelings
lonely fish in alphabet soup

emotion
severs my voice
when I love you / I'm here for you / I'm sorry
I'm craniate, gill-bearing
mouthing in speechless ocean

can't talk too often: friendship is a colander
let you close, you'll see all these holes
and I must dash: unmissable appointments
with the iron lung of solitude

Small talk

Sensory processing disorder

Hey it's great to visit you ow that light the weird smell of your dinner
how have you been birds chirping a bus a barking dog a screaming
neighbourhood child the kettle boiling someone closing a door what's
been happening with you the prickly texture of the couch the washing-
machine running the bitter taste of your brand of tea the temperature
normal for you that burns my mouth oh you want to tell me about Lisa
someone whipper-snipping the sour scent of grass oh she had to go to the
specialist the dishwasher going the electrical hum of the fridge California
California dreamin' on a winter's day oh really an infection the heater
turning on air blowing on me like fingernails down a blackboard your
kids tipping out the Lego box and squabbling the itchy tag on my clothing
your text messages my text messages the washing-machine deafening and
vibrating into pain and here's Beverley O'Connor with another ABC news
update oh do I look as though I'm miles away sorry

Candles Unattended: a clinical history
Dyspraxia, hypotonia

Dyspraxia was called Clumsy Child Syndrome until 1989.

onset is in early childhood and is lifelong

couldn't do what children did
running   climbing   games   sport
so I've never been a child. I watched the Olympics,
longed to be a gymnast, but all I could play at
was ribbon twirling, Mum's long orange grosgrain
sketching limber shapes my body could not emulate.

clumsy children are less well-liked
and have low self-esteem

clumsy with its barrowload of slurs. My given names:
unco, weakling, gawky,
hurry-up, useless. Fruitlessly I practiced
dancing and shooting hoops – picked only once
for netball, where I shut down, stock-still, bewildered.
Ten years of practice to master makeup, so never pretty.

persistent limitations in daily living
little working memory

can't do what adults do
so I've never been an adult. Can't make or fix things.
In danger from knives and ovens.
Can't barbecue or ride a bike, can barely swim
can't pitch a tent, start a gas cooker,
saying *no, thanks* to all those invitations.

fatigue is common, so much extra energy is expended
trying to execute physical movements

the concentration
of   just   walking   swallowing
turning the key in the lock
aiming the hair dryer so as not to incinerate
my hair, my family-joke name Candles Unattended
will I drop the baby, burn it in the bath?

difficulties with walking: slowness,
frequent tripping and bruising

can't walk in a group, outpaced
can't walk and talk. My futile search
for bushwalks which don't have hills; even then
Jedi-mind for the pain.
My hesitancy on grass, on stairs:
bright blooms on elbow and shin.

there is no cure

one reason friendship's hard –
what can we do together?
With you I glide my bike around the streets of Paris
run up mountains
bushwalk
in fantasy. In truth, I watch my every step.

There is always a giraffe
Dyspraxia

Cool as a whale
Mrs Haydon is stepping backwards through water

patient with this small giraffe
who has failed at every sport

all neck and skittery hooves,
large-eyed, patterned with shame.

The giraffe goes down, commanding her eyes
to snap open, kicking the way she's been taught

trying to blow the textbook bubbles
one two three and turn her fine neck

to gasp, so loudly it hurts her ears,
the air that saves her life

for another moment. Again
with fight-or-flight desperation, again

with Mrs Haydon's voice in her head
straight legs, lift your tummy

and her own voice too,
yelling at herself to *do it, do it*

until her legs burn, her nostrils choke,
the certificate floats farther away than Africa

and she knows she will die here, now,
her ears awash with plughole terror

and a fury of incompetence
pounding in her head like a hoofbeat.

Wherever I am, there is always a giraffe
asking if it's worse to drown, or fail.

On whether the earth is flat, round, or there at all

Dyspraxia, dyscalculia

It means not knowing where you are in space,
your arms and legs, your clumsy feet, your hands;
the door, and how you get from here to there,
forgetting how this puppet walks or stands
(exhausting). And, more broadly, means not knowing
where you are in the building, or the street,
the suburb where you've lived for twenty years.
Means driving round till you admit defeat
in a tangle of roads that disconnect,
trying to find the familiar shop or school,
your work, your friends; this often brings on tears.
To travel is to struggle like a fool
because, despite Google maps, the signs,
the sun, you stay as lost as when, aged three,
you let go of your mother's hand and stood
terrified, mouthing shopping-centre pleas;
it's why you take a taxi, not a train,
miss entrances, ask people where things are,
eat in the one cafe you know, again,
because you dare not walk a bridge too far.
It makes the world veer, shift, and be nowhere.
Come here to me. Don't make me meet you there.

Elegy for a fun childhood

Occupational therapy

                    pressure garments forcing my skin
to know less, dumbing it down
                    weighted blankets dissuading my body
from ceaselessly searching for itself
                    headphones replacing the world
with the complex absence anemones hear
                    the scooter-board I row with my hands
floorboard lifeboat, the wheels' headache-roar etched into my parents' prayers
                    therapy music, frequencies inhuman
to repattern twisted violin neurons
                    my small bird-body pushing a chair heavy with dictionaries
up and down the hallway chasing deep-muscle calm
                    my mother hard-pressing hysterical limbs
massaging in our desperation for sleep
                    swallowing a jewel-case of supplements
swallowing my experience, swallowing *just calm down* and *don't make a fuss*
                                but I am a door wide open
to the ocean of lightcolourmovementtalktexturepressuretastebalance
my house is sodden, filled to the ceiling where I thrash
face-up in the air-pocket   this work
my slog
                    child labour
                                life sentence
what I have to do to sit in that flooded classroom tomorrow
where my teacher will say to me
don't you think you could be trying a little bit harder?

Mealanelle

Avoidant/restrictive food intake syndrome (ARFID) in autism

Our eating disorder's off the charts.
Hardly a food gets past our lips.
Instead, we bite down on our hearts.

Our sense of texture, taste, departs
from normal. Nearly all food flips
to feel repulsive, off the charts.

Our mothers tried nutritious starts:
they shouted, force-fed, hands on hips.
Now they bite down on their hearts.

When one fad ends, another starts –
one or two foods the rest eclipse.
Our grocery bill is off the charts

when Mum is filling shopping carts
with pricey brands of sea salt chips.
Soothed, we bite down on our hearts.

Mum's friends think we're spoiled upstarts –
that's put an end to dinner trips.
Our eating disorder's off the charts

and less-than-perfect body parts
attract girl bullies' verbal whips;
shamed, we bite down on our hearts.

Our pediatrician taps growth charts.
Our mums beg us for merest sips.
Our eating disorder's off the charts,

sad mums are counting poos and farts
while our anaemic blood-nose drips.
Starved, we bite down on our hearts.

Unseen, this daily martial art
we fight to keep on living, grips.
Our eating disorder's off the charts.
Weeping, we bite down on our hearts.

Night vision: apology to a late-diagnosed daughter
Autism

for jamming the toothbrush into your mouth while you cried and fought
your body being entered for setting you up to fail with reward charts you
could only manage for a day for scolding and enforcing consequences
for denying you pocket money trying to make you do chores you could
never do and didn't understand for forcing food between your lips and
frightening you into swallowing for the calm lengthy reasoning I did with
you as to why you should do better for feeling choked that you needed
every inch of my personal space all the time for praising you when you'd
done something right when praise just made you more anxious for
towering over your tiny body and pointing my finger as I shouted for not
realising after you'd gotten off a chair thirty times and I'd put you back
on thirty times that there was a learning problem not a discipline one for
bellowing at you to go to sleep sleep sleep for putting you back in your
bed over and over like Supernanny said until you were beside yourself
and so was I for denying you screen time which made you start peeling
skin off yourself in agitation for pushing you into the bath and out of the
bath and telling you to stop whingeing as I did your hair with the brush
you howled was sharp and the hairdryer you howled was loud for putting
back on you the clothes and shoes you perpetually pulled off for losing
sympathy about your endless injuries for never telling my friends that
you bit your mouth till it bled and wiped the blood on the walls and that
your ceaseless anxiety had worn you to a bag of bones and that I walked
on eggshells instead of enjoying my parenting for leaving you wailing in
time-out for anything I did to you to assuage my own distress for being
a new parent who had no language for what you were, for being slow to
see you, I'm sorry. You are parallax, shoal, diaspora. You are percipience,
cloud-measurer, reverie. You are love-scar, bioluminescence.

Outside

It's common for autistic girls to make friends with boys, with whom social interactions are often clearer.

At age six, we got it – our stick-flimsy bodies
and Coke-bottle glasses, though unpopular,
were a gift: the tools of an intellectual life.
Cross-legged on the school library carpet, Darren and I
read encyclopedias and *National Geographic* at lunchtimes,
took notes on common fossils of the Cretaceous period,
tested each other on how many million miles
it was to get to Neptune or Ursa Minor;
stayed glassed in, like strange exhibits,
while outside kids leapt and wrangled,
yelled for keepings-off and chasings.

This despite our proud no-nonsense surnames –
both families deep-rooted in the country town
with proper jobs: his Pop the butcher, mine the barber.
We deserved genes for footy, hard work, strong beer.

I'd go to Darren's place with armloads of books
when I had the courage – his brother bit and scratched
like a tortured cat. They labelled him allergic
and sentenced him to soy milk and rice cakes –
these days it would be Ritalin –
and his mum was just as unnerving,
always on the brink of wits'-end tears.
Mostly we read in the tiny school library
in New Road (next up from Old Road),
horizons branching into esoteric maps.

I should have seen it then,
how many million miles away we were.
We do what's left to us.
Darren's still studying: geology.
I'm writing, head down, glassed in,
glancing up only occasionally
at that inscrutable chaos
past the door.

Thirteen ways of looking at a waxwork girl

In Ehlers-Danlos Syndrome, common with autism, all tissues apart from the bones are too weak. The body hurts all the time, and it's hard to stand up or walk.

crash-test
dummy

stretched
canvas

tenderised
meat

rusty
hinge

jenga

sparkler

soggy
weetbix

bruised
peach

-itis

mock-up

fixer-upper

wallflower

old child

Autistic girl as Beaker the Muppet

Blown up, electrocuted, eaten
by monsters, afflicted with side effects,
my hair stays in the red, my eyes are peeled.

I long ago ditched words. My cries of *meep*
pass for small talk – anyway, their laughter
covers anything I might have said.

Not the type you want to chill out with –
my nerdy mind and danger-radar
make me no-one's good-time friend.

I was made for this,
my calling to embody fresh distress.
To feel too much, turn up for it again.

The autistic girls' mothers to astronaut Mike Collins

How could other parents understand
she can't regulate, can't dress, screams in wind?
Their girls touch down, their modules steady, small footsteps
breaking the moon-sand's surface, their milestones
cosmic miracles of the ordinary. We long
for their basic okayness, their assumption
that the whole team will walk on the moon,
get to jump, twirl in the applause, treasure the video.
Like you, Mike, we come so close,
our deficiency the only explanation. We know your loneliness,
how compared to the others you have so little to say.
With you we calculate, re-check trajectories,
live cold in shadow, looking but never landing,
punch once more into the unyielding switches
our daily goals: feeding, bathing, schooling,
and sail again around the curve into black,
orbiting our peers, worlds from it all.

What I know about nights

Delayed sleep phase disorder

They arrest the open eye.

They are measured on a parabola of hopefulness.

They study my schedule, throw it away.

They sleep with other people, of whom I am jealous.

They evade questions about morning.

They tell me I'm their special girl.

They pass me around, one to the other.

They crave my listening ear.

They swell in my body as pain.

They are the darkness that's dread, the darkness that's light, the darkness
  I swallow.

They are an hourly gamble, losing, losing.

They suckle from my tomorrow.

They exclude me, occlude me,

and in excruciating dawn

leave my time-skinned body

asleep through another day

and missing you, your world of sunlit living.

And night by day

Narcolepsy

...day by night and night by day oppressed,
And each, though enemies to either's reign,
Do in consent shake hands to torture me...
– Sonnet 28, William Shakespeare

The magma field is inhospitable, stark.
It's not the blackout, the hand that slips
from the wheel, the line-crossing veer.
I stole a rock from a smoking volcano.

Not the blackout, the hand that slips
with the knife, but a crippling need to sleep.
I stole a rock from a smoking volcano,
breaking the rules, clenching my fingers tight

as if around a knife. Crippling, sleep
jetlags my days, a yawning crevasse.
Breaking the rules, clenching my fingers tight,
I try to explain to another employer

that sleep jetlags, each eye a dark crevasse –
no waking, or working, until after noon.
I try to explain to another employer
the sadness of seeing no sunrises.

She's apathetic, won't work until afternoon.
Then the turn: sleepless till four in the morning,
never a sunrise except inversely, vexed time
spent driving in the dark, others in bed –

no sleep until four in the morning,
no gain in stealing that stone.
I spent the flight back gripping it
the way I long to hold days, nights:

never mine, that night-light yellow wellness.
Wearily I go, count my eked-out hours.
I hear of days and nights, that flourishing land.
Magma falls from my hand, my brand-mark.

I didn't get the memo
ADHD

or I get the memo and lose it
or I read the memo too quickly and misunderstand it
or I understand the memo but miss that it refers to today
or I go to another room looking for what I need for the memo but don't
    know why I'm there
or I gather everything the memo tells me I need, then leave it in the
    hallway
or I put the things in the car, then leave them in the car
or I go to wear what the memo tells me to but I've washed it and forgotten
    to hang it out
or I remember the memo in the toilet but forget it at the desk
or I write the memo on a sticky note and put some books over it
or I text myself the memo but don't check my messages
the memo slides like oil through my fingers
the memo is chiselled onto an ice sculpture, melting
the memo is written on spinning plates
the memo becomes butterflies and I have no net
the memo practises social distancing

[working memory]

I wake as a missing person, years
written in silt below the wave.
I infer from what clues appear.
The slate is a slate and not a page.

Memory is a room swept clear,
a gaping, empty animal cage.
I won't recall I was ever here.
The slate is a slate and not a page.

Conversations in one ear
and out the other, gone. I stage
recollection, live with fear.
The slate is a slate and not a page.

You'll read my blanks as lack of care,
shared history wiped as friendships age.
Here's why I cannot bring you near.
The slate is a slate and not a page.

Can't Keep House Woman

Sensory distress, dyspraxia, pathological demand avoidance, ADHD

Can't Keep House Woman
can't have friends over
they step over half-empty plates and glasses
unfolded washing and animal litter
filthy   pig sty   how can anyone live like that
Can't Keep House Woman says
sorry sorry sorry
her shame aflame

Can't Keep House Man
has all his friends over
they step over half-empty plates and stubbies
dust and power cords
it's a bachelor pad!
They play Playstation
eat from pizza boxes   laugh
slap him on the back
thanks for a great night, mate

Limbic Airways Flight AUT101
Autism with ADHD

Welcome on board! My name is Cognitive Confusion. Our captain today is Executive-Function Impairment, and our co-pilot is Memory Dysfunction. With us are our wonderful cabin crew, Overwhelm and Self-Fulfilling Prophecy, who can come to you at any time. In your seat pocket you will find a safety card: the card is in your own handwriting and includes instructions for getting dressed, taking medications, paying bills and eating regularly. Even though you may have flown with us many times before, you will still need to refer to these instructions on every flight. Your seat belt should now be fastened tightly around your mouth, keeping others safe from your social deficits. The complimentary headphones will deliver a stream of invective, inaudible to those around you. The cabin will remain pressurised throughout the flight; this sensory pressure will be relentless. For much of the day we will need to fly squares around turbulence, during which you may access, on our inflight entertainment, a game where you throw tasks into a huge bucket and are unable to prioritise them. You will likely feel sick over what you are not accomplishing; please use the bags provided. Please note that smoking is not permitted aboard the aircraft, nor is relief from any addictive substance. Penalties apply for asking that others accommodate your disability; please note that these excuses must not be used during the flight, particularly if you are travelling for work. You should be familiar with the brace position and the fetal position, as you will find yourself using these frequently. If you become so distressed that it becomes necessary to leave the aircraft, there are two exits through the forward doors, leading to embarrassment; two exits over the wings, leading to the sea of self-recrimination; and two exits at the rear of the aircraft, leading to isolation. If oxygen is required, masks will drop from the ceiling above you; it is essential that you wear a mask to access the flow of social acceptance. Emotional decompression will occur without warning. This is a non-stop service travelling from waking to broken sleep.

The autistic hermit crab resists excursions

Speak not to me your nonsense
about *relaxing getaways*, that wholesale ripping-away
of my every reference point, integument.

To shed sensory security is to walk skinless
peppered by the grit of shot, stabbed by birds.

Let me rest on familiar furniture, know myself covered,
bring in my legs, my over-stimulated eye-stalks.

My sleep is attuned to the glow of my streetlight,
scent of blanket, precise curve of mattress.

You who would get me out of the house,
how adventurous you'd feel
were I to strip you, take to you with a peeler.

Stillanelle
The pathological demand avoidance (PDA) profile of autism

Kiss goodbye every project that you planned.
As soon as you have purpose, and devise
a task, it's now a trigger: a demand.

Demands freeze you. The moment you command
yourself to act, this hex will paralyse:
too anxious to enact the joys you'd planned,

each step gargantuan, and on quicksand.
Lie in this maze bricked up before your eyes,
struggle to breathe – yes, breathing's a demand.

Why can't you muscle forward, take command?
Become more frozen with repeated tries.
You can't push on, push through. Only unplanned

zigzagging is possible, the merest strand
of agency in reach: whatever lies
outside of urgent, whatever is no demand.

There's moments you can take yourself in hand
and force yourself, but that will penalise
with days of sleep, as, bankrupt, you crash-land.

For women, there's a tide of reprimands:
the dirty floors, the fridge where the meat lies
rotting – cleaning, cooking, all demands.

The more significant, the more it's banned.
Can't call your dearest aunt before she dies.
Can't chase your passion, find your promised land.

It's not a problem people understand
or forgive, when you can't socialise
or make it to the office on demand.

You're hemmed in, feeling anxiousness expand
and overpower, press, immobilise
until you weep, relinquish what was planned.

This throttling paradox, this inverse land –
it dessicates the heights to which you'd rise.
Kiss goodbye every project that you planned.
There's more to tell – but speaking's a demand.

Shaky underpinnings
Dysautonomia, panic disorder

Instead of strength,
this tickertape of error messages:

too little/too much
hot/cold   in/out   heart's thud.

Hand-addressed distress,
precision pain –

weakness my inherited land.
Trekking the boundaries of quagmire,

how to construct a shelter
in a marsh's connective tissue

where serpents nest, waterfowl
cry down dissecting nerves,

plovers peck at eyes.
My swelled wetland body, my rice-paper skin

translucent in sunlight, and burning.
Where to make camp

when I slump into seizure,
when friends gently disrobe me

chock my body for the quake?
King's horses, king's men   they couldn't

and can't. Can't (my touchstone)
sleep, wake, eat, stand, breathe,

lust, turn up. I am the friend
whom the kind have given up asking.

And now, cardiac panic shrill in my ears –
my diving bell breached, and filling.

The shamed body addresses its owner

Autistic burnout, dyspraxia, fibromyalgia, chronic fatigue

I did not ask to be given to you
already broken, bits rattling in the box.

There was no kintsugi craftsman
to lovingly mend me with gold
in the seventies.

At two, my inability to catch
presaged much. At fifteen, the hard smack
of my body on the orange lino confirmed it.

I failed to leave home to backpack.
At nineteen, it took my mother
to pull a jumper over my head.
I bought plastic cutlery – not as painful to lift.

By the nineties, real women
wore power suits, did step aerobics
and made up their minds to get over cancer.
Running boardrooms, they ran away from us.

So what could you talk to your friends about,
what was the argot?
You got angry, disavowed me. I waited:
you couldn't live without me.

You dressed me to look like the others.
Weekend at Bernie's
seemed funny at the time. People said
I looked like Nicole Kidman, had a bright future.
We both knew better.

It was only at night, when all was still,
that you listened: we made poems together.

And now, your daughter diagnosed,
you speak me back into being,
apply like honey to wounds
language to each deficit.

You say my names: but will you introduce me
to your friends? Are you still ashamed –

Illanelle

Due to many physical and mental health conditions, autistic people live much shorter lives.

The tree grew tall, but failed to bloom.
I hide it from you, cope on my own.
My civil war will defeat me soon.

The lifelong illness is auto-immune,
bodily war in the first seed sown.
The tree grew tall, but failed to bloom.

My friends are looking at Europe's moon;
it hurts to walk from my car to my home.
This private war will defeat me soon.

Nobody knows I sleep past noon,
my Western shame: the bludger's clone.
The tree looks tall, but cannot bloom.

Termites chatter in every room.
Too weak to go out, too tired for the phone,
my daily war will exile me soon.

I enjoy what I can, though futures loom –
I'm a warming earth, a riven stone.
The tree grew tall, but would not bloom.
My civil war will release me soon.

The head-stacking caterpillar answers the question *how are you?*

Female autism, autistic shutdown

How

Happy to be doing this activity with you, while I get worse from doing it. Do you know how I split my face and head off, wrest it free of my distressed body, reattach it with filament, make it smile? Do you know how this unstitching dichotomy, this severing of wellness from happiness, is done in the psyche's inky cocoon? People feel unwell, they take the day off and get better. I never get better, so I can't keep waiting for that: I do what brings me joy. I won't go home after this and cook dinner, reply to emails, have a shower, make lunch for tomorrow. I'll go to bed, and in bed, I'll experience distressing symptoms. I'm a many-legged complexity, a walking trade-off, silken, elegant, ruthless. This head looks fine.

are

I can't listen, think and speak all at the same time. I can only do one of those things. I need a few seconds to understand what you've said, especially if there's background noise, and then a few more to discover what I genuinely think about what you've said, if I can do that at all in this sensory environment. If I take those seconds, there will be a long gap after you speak, and because I'm a woman (bubbly and bright), you'll feel that I don't have much interest in you, that I don't find you engaging. I know this from having people quite literally walk away. To fill that gap, here's echolalia, my speech and body language from your energy, my return of your serve, trigger-happy talk, sound-bites, a trite dip into facile phrases that may not even be true for me. My mood, my lexicon are your mirror, whether you're up, down, quick or slow. So, strangely, how I seem – how I "am" – will be almost entirely about how you are. This head is empty, chill with exoskeletal echoes.

you

Ah yes, "me" – the titanic range between my high functioning and my low functioning. The career me is smart, quick, capable. The impaired executive-function me is confused and disoriented. The intellectual me is happily going down a deep-learning rabbit hole. The demand-avoidant me is in bed, in terror, in the fetal position. The poet me is delightedly writing. The Ehlers-Danlos me is hurting all over. The narcoleptic me is exhausted to the point of pain. The mother me is wise. The social-avoidant me can't return calls and worries that no one will keep liking me. The me that worships is steady and deep. The dangerously credulous me gets abused and can't know that it won't happen again. The singing me is joyful. The uncoordinated me is dangerous to myself and others. The sensory-avoidant me struggles to get into the shower and is immobilised by a hair or a speck of dust and sick with fear that she might become unable to clean at all. The mental health me is feeling hopeless over all this and had to be talked away from the metaphorical ledge to connect with the world today, clinging in grit. All these mes are present, and I've had to precisely measure them, bargain with them, wade through their head-swamping wet concrete just to get out of the house. Which heads will I tell you about? Only the good ones? Then I know you don't really know me. And which of the bad ones won't you find alarming, too much information? None of them? That's right.

?

Which of the social settings in which we see each other would be an appropriate place to tell you all this? So I lie.

What I can do when I'm in autistic shutdown, which will probably happen after you've seen me today

How are you?
Alexithymia, dysphoria, depression in autism

People say *fine, busy, tired,*
none of which approximate
the sight when I lift the plank of myself
and find it crawling with slaters, rimed
with acrid mould, a bedlam of decomposition
in which nothing can be read.
I drop it down again:
not something I want to touch.

Put words to this babel? I tried
but lost all bearings in the intricacy.
And you were horrified by what you heard, told me
it surely wasn't that bad.

A child, I learned the right word – *good* –
and said it reflexively, self-checkout saying
please take your items. The word
passes clean through me,
an empty radio wave. I ache for terms
from neurochemistry, zoology, science fiction
but when at last they come
      alexithymia   dysphoria   depression attack
the words carry no meaning to you, dropping off the cliff
of your mystified expression.
I can only keep on doing
what girls are trained to do,

painting the same four letters
on the plank's sunlit top.

How autism may present in adult female siblings

I wear high heels   she wears men's clothing
I drive a Saab   she drives an old Land Cruiser

we live with
sensory processing disorder ADHD anxiety narcolepsy demand avoidance

I need minimalism   she needs dogs and ferrets
I relax in fine restaurants   her therapy is bottling fruit

we run from
friendships tax-returns appointments bills shops goodbyes

I mask stress with makeup   she gets tattoos
I won't have even my ears pierced   she pierces everything

we share
specialists diagnoses cognitive strategies weighted blankets homeopathy

I'm a cat owner   she's a wildlife carer
I have faith   she has theories

we like
text-chatting literary puns Benedict Cumberbatch Seven of Nine

independently we get blue hair in the same week

I can't have dirty hands   she plants things
my Ehlers-Danlos Syndrome makes my body hurt   hers puts her in hospital

                          we text
                   from our respective beds

I battle my clutter   she lives with hers
I'm a hothouse flower   she's steampunk

                 addiction sings to both of us

I write about my difficulties   she studies special needs
I pretend to have it all together   she goes to the psych ward

                       we are drawn
                    to the wrong people

I cower   she fights
I fake   she lies

                     pity our mother

Materials handling sheet for an autistic meltdown

Erasure from article, *[Nuclear] Core Meltdown – an overview*, ScienceDirect

there is a hazard of melt   as well as that of a steam explosion in the head

due to the absence of   proper configuration

when the battery power is used up

tripped due to high pressure in the suppression chamber

the chain reaction is not controlled   complete loss of cooling source

station blackout   containment failure

the explosion

melt could arrive in the head

in the form of several concurrent jets

the head contains a lot of water

and the interaction of melt and water lead to fragmentation

a period of no cooling for at least six and a half hours

with a large jet there may be

ablation of the vessel

graphite may catch fire   huge cloud of particles and vapour

all personnel were evacuated from a large region surrounding

these are highly complex and daunting challenges

because of the difficulties involved in making precise predictions

this study has not investigated the potential consequences

this region has become an experiment on natural recovery

Yes

Suggestibility and situational mutism in female autism

Listen
as the doctor tells us we are not autistic
but depressed or a borderline personality we are saying yes
before megalithic medical power we are saying yes as the specialist
puts us on medication for schizophrenics
we are saying yes as the headmaster tells us our children
are not disabled enough for teacher's aides we are saying
yes to the exam board that says shorter sessions
and headphones are not reasonable adjustments yes
to the pittance from the suspect employer
yes to the fundraisers and the credit cards
yes to the telemarketer and his solar panels we are saying
yes to the dysfunctional friend who wants all our time and yes
to the homeless man who knows which house we live in
yes to the online catfishers and the predatory dates yes
to the masseur who touches us too far and yes
to the man who just needs a bit of help
to get on his feet and yes we will go to his house
and yes we will hold him and yes
we are soft-bodied and agreeable
perilous though it is

girl brains mean nothing

at once private
and bare   no reference work
on whether to meet the eyes   of Aussie men
how are ya luv   her pear
in the cockatoo's claw

                     girl brains mean nothing

Acca Dacca bawling
from the neighbour's son's ute   his mates
wording him up
    autistic ones
never tell

Miss Diagnosis: how to lose when seeing a specialist

Speak
and they don't see autism.

Don't speak
and they don't hear a problem.

Bring notes of your history
and they see an obsessive.

Bring research
and they see a hypochondriac.

Keep calm
and they see no dysfunction.

Get upset
and they see a drama queen.

Be a woman
and you're just not a credible bloke.

Female autism diagnostic journey

draw attention
draw a blank
draw fire
drawing board

draw on my energy
         money
         doggedness
overdrawn

drawn face
     curtain
     inference
     conclusion

luck of the

end in a

Perennially gaslit, the autistics reject humanity

No support to gentle my exhaustion.
I wrangle through as I wrangle
daily, scantily resourced, MacGyvering my problems
(no doubt I'm feigning them.)

My employment future: forever 2IC –
power positions for the full-time only
and no more Zoom to reach me in bed:
the pandemic's over now.

Everyone so nosey to know
why-can't-you, demanding
tabloid drama, that I bare my underbelly
and let them test it with a foot. Why aren't we terminal,

easy to process? We fit no system, too weird
or not malformed enough.
Doctors' skeptical stares,
Centrelink's razorlike instruments,

support services too busy to call back.
We aren't wanted,
won't be missed. Little wonder
that we shy now at this pillory

go to the insects, plants, land, sky.

Self-portrait as a restrained animal

A few books by women detail the familiar
battle to get to here –
contradicted, mislabeled,
dismissed, laughed at.
Every one of us mystified by our own strange
failings, our tiredness, forever falling through the
gap between two trapezes:
hysterical, the old chestnut
insulting for so many centuries, new medical
journals still wheezing with stereotypes.
Kinder to myself nowadays, given this
lottery of what-deficit-is-presenting-as-
me in any moment, and this Sisyphean second-guessing:
not a thought or word
or impulse can run unchecked – it will be
perhaps inaccurate, perceived as inappropriate, and,
quite likely, be unsafe for a woman. Imagine
reining yourself in over and over,
stopping the sweet horse of your self
taking to the free ground and running.
Unsure, withholding voice and action, without simple
veracity from my senses, what can I enjoy?
When the TV says that autism is a superpower, that it's the new
x-factor in employment, I want to say
you haven't seen my portrait: a
zebra tied to a stake, circling on its shortening leash.

Billanelle

There is no money left, just bills outgoing.
Expenses mount: the cost of being me
is high. Government payments are not growing.

I worked until I had the girls, but going
to school's too hard for their autism. He
(my ex) is deemed to need a set outgoing

amount to live: no maintenance is owing.
Strangely, this amount is not deemed for me
or the girls, and every day they're growing.

Autism assessment: two-and-a-half grand, for knowing
what I already know. All therapies
cost hundreds. Catch-22 of bills outgoing:

insure my contents or my car; stop going
to shops, eat markdown meat, drink cheap-brand tea,
few holidays, no hobbies. Sense my growing

fear about the future, the debts I'm towing:
women need sound plans financially.
No savings, no super, everything outgoing.

I did some casual work – the pay's still owing;
I couldn't send the bill (anxiety).
My mental health? The camel's back is bowing.

NDIS exclusions overflowing:
the medications, naturopathy,
chiro, pool, supplements that keep us going –

they say they're not approved. And never slowing,
the maddening costs of ADHD:
late fees, lost fees, things I can't return, throwing

cash away, the shamefulness of knowing
I can't do better. One catastrophe
away from homelessness or medically going

without. The stress of hand-to-mouth is showing.
Can't eat out with you; thanks for asking me.
There is no money, only bills outgoing.
My disability poverty is growing.

Maslow's Hierautism of Needs

Self-actualisation: to become the most that one can be.

All the best with that.

Esteem: respect, self-esteem, status, recognition, strength, freedom.

Devastated by history of thwarted projects, studies, life paths. Choices made by committee of disorders.

Love and belonging: friendship, intimacy, family, sense of connection.

[Information missing.] Anxiety. Loneliness preferable to misinterpretation and worry. Raising disabled children unsupported.

Safety needs: employment, personal security, resources, health, property.

String of exploitative relationships, under-employed, hounding scant government resources, financially crippled by high health expenses, will never own property, suicide twice the rate of autistic men.

Physiological needs: air, water, food, shelter, sleep, clothing, reproduction.

Breathing, eating, sleep a chaos: distress changeless. Clothing a burr of nerves, this shelter my cave. Don't touch me.

Threnody of the autistic women

*The "lost generation" is the generation born before 1980, the very late
diagnosed adults. There is very little known about adult female autism.
– Tania Marshall, I Am AspienWoman*

generation grown
whingeing lazy weird
flaw-exposure feared
very little known

managing what's shown
functioning at best
then the days of rest
very little known

anxiety-prone
many threads to lose
easily I bruise
very little known

several jobs I've blown
resume's a mess
sensory distress
very little known

friends have mostly flown
think of them so much
hard to keep in touch
very little known

potential never shown
been left on the shelf
have to blame myself
very little known

How have you succeeded despite having autism?

The prefix "aut-" means "self".

At first, I am disauder, distressed auganism. I cannot count on the audinary. Efforts come to naut – I triage, relinquish, harden up: hindsight and forethaut my advisors, flight my reliable last resaut. I am an auphan in this singular authogenesis, autonomous but so hamstrung, my writing my only authodox ability, stamp on my passpaut; I postulate, innovate, medicate, auganise, theorise, rig workarounds auganically. Still, it's not auderly: the sensory onslaut, the social audeal, the mental diatribe – my knitting half-dropped, plans abauted, friendships untended, fences unmended. Swathes of my life that memory will never repaut. Every success is hand-wraut, hard-faut; I still don't know how to ask for suppaut. I am self-taut.

Still I rise: female autism

Do you think I am mistaken
'Cause my label mystifies?
Do you want to contradict me?
I defy the one who tries.

Widen out your definition.
Try my burdens on for size.
I'm a stereotype-breaker
And, like knowledge, I will rise.

I'm the tree encased in concrete.
I'm the wingless bird who flies.
Daily, witness my endeavour –
Singing anthems, I will rise.

I've the might of twenty warriors.
I've the grit to actualise
What small wins are in my power.
Though disabled, still I rise.

Does it give you dissonance
That there are diamonds in my eyes?
I can keep my struggles private
Yet I share my joys, and rise.

I will name truth when I choose to.
I have learned to meet your eyes.
I'll light paths for other women.
Still unfolding, still I rise.

Joy to my world

Neuroplasticity

tablecloth ripped out from under
happiness' crockery
never trusted joy
cross-wired with dread
took years untangling the electricals   but now

                            joy to my world

is my revelation: in life's second half
I'm larking about   letting off
delight's fireworks in cranial sky
jackwiring neurons to sensory bliss
orchestrating razzamatazz

Neurodiverse

I, nervous reed,
ever so ruined.
Our nerves die!
Our seed riven,
severed in our
reveries. Undo?

Deserve in our
derive. No ruse.
Revise, undo re
overused rein.
Never die sour!

Nerved, I rouse,
   unrevised ore,
   due reversion,
   overdue siren.
Endure is over,
over. Nu desire –
redo universe.

For I will consider the delightfulness of my grown daughter
Autism

For at two in the morning she sings Japanese pop
In perfect Japanese. For she designs
Cross-stitch spaghetti earrings, a thing no human has ever attempted.
For she wears what she likes, looking extraordinary.
For she wins science awards and writes a novel like it's easy.
For she knows what she thinks to be right and follows it.
For she speaks to me of *My Little Pony* and *Ninjago*.
For she refuses to ever reverse park.
For she works every week in the judging, fearsome world.
For she bears her maladies with magnificent fortitude.
For she still lays on my bosom, loves me abidingly.
For I will praise and champion her forever.

Now you are eighteen

it doesn't seem right to step into your room
and watch you sleep. I call up your sleep-sweetened face,
how it rested and turned in the half-light
in the bed beside me for so many years,
drawn lashes, cheek's apple, downy line
of hair, its length now your pride,
a hazel waterfall hanging to your waist,
tall, stripling woman, stylish by day in your bright
Japanese blouse and red suede boots
or black jackboots and hoodie, elegant as a new animal,
walking shining and dewdrop pure in the ageing air
of this world. You loved the seesaw, and my legs compensated
for your smallness, boosting you gently up,
then cushioning as you fell back down,
my body at the ready to bear whatever impact
would shield you. And it still is ready, my darling,
as you sit now at the tipping point of those years
and the next eighteen, of loves, and loves lost, perhaps of children.

female aut-ism

fraught-ism
raw-tism
fought-ism
war-tism
thwart-ism
roar-tism
thought-ism
flaw-tism?
taught-ism?
rort-ism?
nought-ism?

daught-ism
soar-tism
more-tism
awe-tism

How to have an autistic friend

See that my scales flash gilt:
the prowess, gift.
Acknowledge the lack in me,
how baffling the lacunae.
Invite me, fit the schedule to me.
If I prefer calling, call. If I prefer texting, text.
If I can't answer, know
I can't answer. If I forget,
remind. Remind anyway. When I can't follow through,
be kind. Remember the iceberg
balancing under this peak,
how intensely I'm thrashing
underwater. See
what can't be seen, like city stars. Give me rest
and more rest, time
and more time. Sweep the path
leading towards my success. Listen
to what I say I can do,
to anything I say. Shield me
from trauma. Laugh
and lighten me, welcome me
when I am present, believe in my verity,
that if I could have, I would have,
and that I wanted and want
to move closer, though quandary
travels with me wherever I go,
though it's here now, in the room.
And know that, in my crenellated mangroves,
my guarded lees, my exoskeletal calm,
this seahorse-soul is lit with love for you.

The autistic woman's self-compassion blessing

Lay down the telephone.
May wheeling birds speak your messages.

Lay down your medical advocacy.
May pink robins nest in your Centrelink forms.

Lay down your twelve-hour productivity.
May your bed be praised, scented with spices.

Lay down your friendship anxieties.
May the words you said be received like bouquets.

Lay down the baggage of completion.
May quokkas carry away your unfinished projects.

Lay down the grout cleaner.
May books and waratah bloom in unswept corners.

Lay down the good mother's drivenness.
May children grow strong by your fountain of loyalty.

Lay down the body shield of silence.
May chosen friends give ear to your simple needs.

Lay down the paper doll of stereotype.
May fierce determination create your singular success.

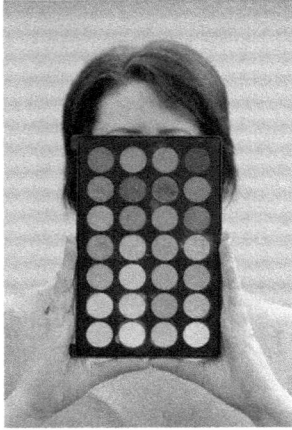

Esther Ottaway is a Tasmanian/lutruwita poet who is autistic and has multiple disabilities, and who is caring for, and has partly home educated, an autistic daughter with multiple disabilities.

Esther's poetry appears in leading Australian and overseas journals including *Rattle* (US), *The Australian* and *The Canberra Times*, and is widely anthologised, notably in University of Queensland Press' *Thirty Australian Poets* and the *Australian Poetry Anthology* series. Esther co-edited *Australian Poetry Journal*'s themed issue, *divergence, relevance*.

Her poems have been shortlisted in the global prizes, the Montreal International, MPU International, Mslexia and Bridport, and among her awards are the Tim Thorne Prize for Poetry and People's Choice in the Tasmanian Literary Awards, the Tom Collins Poetry Prize, the Queensland Poetry Festival Ekphrasis Award and a Varuna Fellowship.

Poems from Esther's first book, *Blood Universe: poems on pregnancy* have been reproduced in national and international anthologies, listed as further reading in *60 Classic Australian Poems*, featured on Radio National and set to music for the Tasmanian Symphony Orchestra.

Her multi-award-winning second book, *Intimate, low-voiced, delicate things*, explores family and its origins, parenthood, love and the loss of love, and has been described as "poetry at its finest, glorious in its vivid imagery, tenderly moving" (Dr Robyn Rowland).

Esther is a recipient of Australia Council for the Arts grants, a former Board member of *Island* magazine, and a former Communications Co-ordinator for the Tasmanian Writers' Centre. She is a member of Arts Tasmania's Expert Register, a National Assessor for Regional Arts Australia, and a poetry tutor of adults with disabilities through the NDIS and Arts Access Australia.

www.ingramcontent.com/pod-product-compliance
Lightning Source LLC
Chambersburg PA
CBHW031004090426
42737CB00008B/671